THREE MASTERS OF THE RENA[ISSANCE]

LEONA[RDO]
MICHELANGELO
RAPHAEL

Claudio Merlo

Illustrations by: S. Boni, L.R. Galante, Sergio

BARRON'S

DoGi

English translation © Copyright 1999
by Barron's Educational Series, Inc.
Original edition © 1999 by DoGi spa, Florence, Italy
Title of original edition: *I tre giganti del Rinascimento*

Italian edition by:
Claudio Merlo
Illustrations by:
Simone Boni, L. R. Galante, Sergio
Editor:
Francesco Milo
Graphic Display:
Sebastiano Ranchetti
Art Director:
Sebastiano Ranchetti
Page make-up:
Giovanni Breschi, Sebastiano Ranchetti
Iconographic Researcher:
Katherine Carlson Forden

English translation by Marion Lignana Rosenberg

All inquiries should be addressed to:
Barron's Educational Series, Inc.
250 Wireless Boulevard
Hauppauge, NY 11788
http://www.barronseduc.com

Library of Congress Catalog Card No. 98-76194

International Standard Book No. 0-7641-0946-4

Printed in Italy
9 8 7 6 5 4 3 2 1

Table of Contents

THE GENIUS OF THE RENAISSANCE

Italian art flourished in the late fifteenth and early sixteenth centuries, when the lives of three of the supreme artistic geniuses of all time intertwined. They are universally known by their first names: Leonardo, Michelangelo, and Raphael.

Many important historians have wondered how it was that three artistic giants happened to live at the same time, surrounded by numerous other masters of similar caliber. No definitive answer is possible. We can, however, seek to know and understand as much as possible about that great period of art and culture known as the High Renaissance, entering the most exclusive halls of power and the workshops of master artists, and exploring the spirit of the times and the historic events that formed the background

The golden florin
Decorated with the motifs of John the Baptist (the patron saint of Florence) and the lily (the symbol of Florence), the florin was one of the strongest currencies of its time.

THE CRADLE OF THE RENAISSANCE
Florence, in central Italy, was the birthplace of a great artistic movement in the fifteenth century. Economic prosperity, a strong work ethic, political stability, and a class of ambitious merchants and bankers all favored the arts and helped support the great workshops, like the one for the construction of the cupola of the *Duomo* (cathedral) of Santa Maria del Fiore.

of their lives. At the end of the 1400s, the contemporaries of these three giants were well aware of their importance. Leonardo, Michelangelo, and Raphael were quickly sought out by the lords of Renaissance Italy and, in the case of Leonardo, by the kings of neighboring France, as well. Their stories intertwine with those of the most important figures of their time and play themselves out in the richest, most ambitious courts and cities. The three giants were born in a relatively small geographic area, though a good number of years apart. The first to appear on the scene was Leonardo.

Country life

On April 15, 1452, in Vinci—a small Tuscan town just outside Florence—

The *Duomo*
Arnolfo di Cambio (c. 1240–c. 1302) started construction of the cathedral of Santa Maria del Fiore. Giotto (1267–1337), who designed the *campanile* (belltower), subsequently took charge of the workshop. Work was completed in 1436, with the closing of the cupola.

Leonardo was born, the eldest son of *ser* Piero di Antonio Da Vinci, a brilliant notary who enjoyed excellent relations with the most important families in the area around Florence. Leonardo was an illegitimate child: his mother, Caterina, a peasant girl in the service of the Da Vinci household, never married *ser* Piero. In fact, shortly after Leonardo's birth, Caterina was given in marriage to Antonio del Vacca, a furnaceman; she was forced to move away from her son, spending the rest of her life in nearby San Pantaleo. Leonardo's birth provoked neither scandal nor shame: the little boy was welcomed warmly into his grandfather Antonio's rich household, where he lived with his father and uncle Francesco.

Like many Tuscan towns, Vinci is set into a hill, from which one can see a landscape dense with olive trees and vineyards, surrounded by forests of oaks and chestnuts. In Leonardo's time, human labor did not disfigure the land; instead, it exalted its agrarian beauty. Leonardo spent the first fifteen years of his life in these surroundings, in an atmosphere of great freedom and serenity. With his beloved uncle Francesco, he observed the work of the peasants, who became his friends. Leonardo's thoughts turned to them again in his later years: a tireless designer of instruments and machines, he created mechanical oil presses, "straight-line" plows, and grain mills.

Leonardo's birthplace
Leonardo was born in Anchiano, which belonged to his mother's family and was just outside Vinci. Leonardo left Anchiano to live in the Da Vinci household.

VINCI
A rural community between Montalbano and Medio Valdarno, its name derives from the wicker *(vinchi)* that was braided on the banks of the stream named Vincio.

The halls of power
The former castle of the Guidi counts served as headquarters for the representatives of the Florentine republic. The church of Santa Croce is nearby.

His father's home
The palazzetto of the Da Vinci, who were notaries as well as producers of artistic ceramics (in Baccereto), landowners, and property owners.

Leonardo's uncle Francesco, loving and somewhat madcap, was his first teacher. Young Leonardo learned how to observe nature and follow the flight of birds by eye; he also studied the basics of drawing, for which he had a natural gift. Memories of the natural vistas of his childhood were never far from his mind: far-away landscapes, like those that can be seen from the castle of Vinci, appeared frequently in his paintings.

In Florence

One day, when Leonardo was a teenager, his life changed dramatically. His father had become an increasingly important man, and was spending more and more time in Florence. He continued to work as a notary, and also participated in city politics as part of the powerful Medici household. In 1565 he moved there permanently, married a woman of his own social class, and in 1567 called his son to Florence. Until that time, Leonardo had lived in the country, albeit in the heart of Tuscany, frequently traveling to such nearby cities as Empoli and Pistoia, where he saw important artists and works of art.

A youthful landscape
Leonardo's first effort was a portion of Verrocchio's painting *The Baptism of Christ.* Seascapes with rocks appeared even in his very last paintings.

The Arno valley

Many believe that this drawing, the very first attributed to Leonardo, depicts the castle of Vinci and the Arno valley.

La Gioconda

Even in the most famous painting in the world (at left), Leonardo set Mona Lisa against a landscape filled with rocks and water.

Vegetation

A realistic rendition of an iris, from the painting entitled *The Virgin of the Rocks*. Leonardo was a keen observer of nature from earliest childhood and depicted natural elements masterfully all his life.

The cupola of the Duomo
From the surrounding hills of Florence, the city seems to crouch beneath the gigantic cupola of the *Duomo*, the largest in the world when it was built by Filippo Brunelleschi at the request of the professional and artistic guilds.

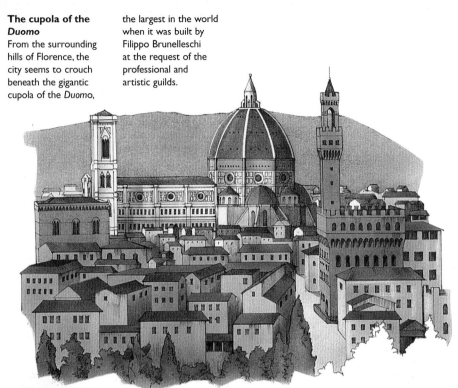

 In Florence, though, he found himself immersed in an environment without equal in the world, then and throughout the fifteenth century. When Leonardo arrived, Florence was in the midst of its Golden Age. In the 1400s its civic, cultural, and artistic flowering reached the highest point in its glorious and tumultuous history. Though two centuries earlier it had grown to its greatest size and attained unsurpassed prosperity and importance in the economy of Western Europe, Florence enjoyed a long period of political stability in the fifteenth century, guided first by the guilds *(corpo-*

razioni) and then, gradually (and unofficially) by the rich bankers of the Medici family, its republican institutions enduring in form only. Peace and wealth favored advanced studies that aimed to recapture the values and the artistic forms of classical Greek and Roman culture, giving rise to the movement known as Humanism. Florence, though, already enjoyed a position of preeminence: in the late thirteenth and early fourteenth centuries, it was the city where Giotto, the founder of "modern" European painting, resided.

In the basilica of Santa Croce, Leonardo admired Giotto's frescoes on

Florentine frescoes
Starting in the Middle Ages, Florentine painters mastered the technique of *buon fresco:* the application of paint to freshly plastered walls.

The great innovation of Florentine fresco painters was the creation of pictorial spaces that seem to reproduce the depth of real space. Giotto, the first great master, after traveling throughout Italy between 1315 and 1325, frescoed two chapels in the basilica of Santa Croce (above, *The Resurrection of Drusiana*).

About a hundred years later, Tommaso Cassai, known as Masaccio (1401–1428), frescoed the Brancacci chapel in the Chiesa del Carmine (below, *The Tribute*).

THE EARLY RENAISSANCE

In Florence, architects and sculptors specialized in works for public spaces: this allowed for greater freedom in experimenting with new artistic "languages."

A LEADER

Donato di Niccolò, known as Donatello (c. 1386–1466) was a pupil of Ghiberti and Brunelleschi (1377–1446). He applied the technique of perspective to bas-reliefs.

Nanni di Banco
(1373–1421)
Four coronati. The figures are life-size.

Orsanmichele
The fourteen statues in the niches were created between 1410 and 1428. Some are in marble, and others in bronze.

Lorenzo Ghiberti
(1378–1455)
Saint Matthew.
The statue is cast in
bronze and measures
106.3" (270 cm) high.

Donatello
Saint George
He stands solidly on the
earth, his feet planted
firmly on the ground, his
face energetic and intent.
12' 4.8" (378 cm) high,
the marble statue was
commissioned by the
armourers' guild.

the life of Saint Francis: they were among the works that marked a turning point in the history of painting, with their realistic depiction of people, settings, and objects. Leonardo visited another important monument in the heart of Florence: an old warehouse converted into the church of Orsanmichele, whose exterior walls contained fourteen niches in which, by order of the *Comune* (municipality), the thriving guilds that directed the civic and economic life of the city placed fourteen statues dedicated to their respective patron saints. It was (and remains) a splendid exhibit, a kind of museum before its time. The major Florentine sculptors of the early fourteenth century—Ghiberti, Nanni di Banco, and the great Donatello—showed that Florentine art had already surpassed Giotto, its innovative master, in the quest for realism. In and around Florence, Leonardo also had access to the works of two giants of the early fifteenth century: the architect Filippo Brunelleschi, and the painter Masaccio.

FLORENTINE WORKSHOPS

His father wanted him to be a notary, but Leonardo was drawn to the various activities of the master artists. Verrocchio welcomed him to his workshop, the ideal place for those who dreamed of becoming artists, inventors, and scientists.

Like all young men from well-bred, educated families, Leonardo devoted his time to studying grammar, geometry, mathematics, and music. He played the lyre very well, but he was most interested in the numerous techniques practiced in the workshops of Florence, whose masters were goldsmiths, sculptors, and painters—artists skilled at picking out the right piece of wood for their paintings and at personally casting their own statues. Most Florentine workshops were successful businesses that filled a variety of orders, ranging from the crafting of furniture or simple decorations for crests to the creation of important altar pieces and fresco cycles that the master and his apprentices would carry out in churches.

A successful workshop was a self-sufficient work group whose members were willing to travel and work as an efficient team in the great *cantieri* (or work sites). The workshops also served as schools for promising young men, whose families initially paid for their room, board, and instruction.

The master artist taught his youngest pupils how to prepare glues, paints, and gessoes. An apprentice generally entered a workshop at the age of 12 or 13.

Antonio Pollaiolo
He lived from 1431 to 1498 and completed his greatest painting, *The Martyrdom of Saint Sebastian*, in 1475.

Andrea Verrocchio
Head of Saint Jerome (1460).
Very few of Verrocchio's paintings have survived.

A YOUNG MASTER
Verrocchio (1435–1480)
was only about 30 when
Piero da Vinci entrusted his
son Leonardo to him. In the
entry to the workshop, death
masks were on display, which
Verrocchio used to create using
gesso mixed with tepid water.

The influential *ser* Piero had no difficulty persuading Andrea di Cione, known as Verrocchio, to accept his son, even though Leonardo was already 17, a very advanced age for joining a workshop as an apprentice: Leonardo's talent was truly exceptional. In 1469, Verrocchio's workshop, along with Pollaiolo's, was the most successful in Florence. A leading institution in the cultural life of Florence in the fifteenth century, Verrocchio's workshop was a place of fundamental importance in the history of art because many of the

LEONARDO
From the courtyard of the workshop, near a machine, the young Leonardo observed the meeting between Verrocchio and his "rival," Pollaiolo.

Perugino
A native of Umbria, he worked in terra-cotta.

Master artists
Seated to the left of Verrocchio, Antonio Benci, known as

Antonio del Pollaiolo, had rediscovered the classical world's love for figures in dynamic poses.

The oven
Workshops had a foundry for bronze with a stone oven, an iron cupola, canal vents, and a runner for casting.

The lavabo
Two workers assemble the marble components of the wash basin for the church of Santo Spirito in Florence.

Botticelli and Ghirlandaio
Though very young men, both already had their own workshops.

most important Renaisance artists spent time there.

What is Florentine art of the fifteenth century?

The artistic revolution set in motion by Giotto in the fourteenth century and carried on by Florentine sculptors of the early fifteenth century became more sharply defined thanks to Brunelleschi, who created linear perspective, which is the technique for representing figures, settings, and entire scenes in such a way that the spectator believes they are taking place in a real environment, represented in three dimensions: height, width, and depth.

The work of Brunelleschi and Donatello gave rise in Florence to the great cultural and artistic phenomenon known as the Renaissance. Masaccio was quick to apply the newly revealed laws of perspective, as was Beato (Fra) Angelico (1378–1455) and, soon thereafter, Filippo Lippi (1406–1469), Paolo Uccello (1397–1475), and many other painters. Their teachers, training, and experiences differed, though all had in common tremendous skill in drawing, and an awareness of its fundamental importance in the creation of realistic images in painting. Florence did not lack for painters keenly interested in coloristic

Paints
The first phase of apprenticeship: grinding pigments.

DRAWING
Live models were used for
figure drawings and for faces.
Mannequins were used for
drawings of draped material,
which took days and days of
patient, meticulous work.

effects, including Domenico Veneziano (c. 1410–1461), the teacher of the great Piero della Francesca (c. 1416–1492). However, it was the subtle, masterful use of line that prevailed in Florentine painting of the fifteenth century and characterized even younger artists, some of whom studied with Verrocchio and among whom Sandro Botticelli (1445–1510) and Filippino Lippi (c. 1457–1504) stand out.

Runners
Once the wax statue was completed, wax rods were added: when the time came to cast the statue, the rods served as runners for the bronze and as air vents.

Burying the mold
The mold was buried to prevent the extreme heat of the melted bronze from causing an explosion.

Sculpting in bronze
The sculptor first created a model in clay, then made a copy by applying a layer of wax over an iron mannequin. The thickness of the wax corresponded to the thickness of the metal.

Removing the mold

After allowing the bronze to cool, workers removed the mold, breaking it with hammers and chisels. At that point, the statue was in rough form, with its runners and air vents still exposed.

Melting the wax

The mold was heated in an oven, so that the wax would melt and be drawn out. An opening was created between the external mold and the mannequin, which would be filled with molten bronze, poured into the mold from the furnace via an opening in the shape of a funnel.

Andrea del Verrocchio

David (c. 1465).

Raising the cage

The flasks that would surround the mold were forged on an anvil. Strong ropes and a winch were used to raise and move the mold.

Andrea del Verrocchio, with Lorenzo di Credi and Leonardo, *The Baptism of Christ* (1472–1475).

TEMPERA AND OIL

Flemish painters had introduced the technique of oil painting some years before. In *The Baptism of Christ,* the angel is painted in oil, while the rest of the painting is in tempera.

"The devil's hand"

Leonardo was left-handed. In later years, he usually wrote from right to left.

Leonardo's earliest works

The workshops of the late Middle Ages and the Early Renaissance functioned to some extent like a modern architectural studio or craft workshop: through teamwork. Today we usually think of a painter's work as a solitary creative pursuit, but this was not the case in Verrocchio's workshop. The master artist did his part—the most important and difficult part, to be sure—but a large work of art was usually created through the *combined* efforts of workshop members. When Verrocchio's workshop was commissioned, for example, to create a large painting depicting *The Baptism of Christ*, the master had Leonardo execute the head of the angel on the left and the landscape in the background. It was the first important proof of the young artist's talent, and legend has it that Leonardo's brilliance led Verrocchio to give up painting. In 1472, Leonardo joined the *compagnia di San Luca*, to which painters belonged, but he continued to work with Verrocchio, who taught Leonardo to prepare his paintings carefully, with detailed, systematic studies accompanied by notes and preparatory drawings of the subjects the young artist had chosen. In 1476, when he was 24, Leonardo left Verrocchio's workshop. He was soon noticed by Lorenzo de' Medici (1449–1492), an elegant, learned patron of the arts and the political leader of the city. Leonardo painted *The Annunciation* and began a long, tortuous phase of study and preparation for *The Adoration of the Magi*.

LEONARDO IN MILAN

The arts and sciences held no secrets for Leonardo: he offered his expertise in mechanics, hydraulics, architecture, painting, sculpture, and war to the lords of Milan. He also created theatrical sets for the splendid entertainments of the court.

Leonardo's life once again underwent a dramatic change. Lorenzo the Magnificent carried out diplomatic relations with other Italian lords in original, creative ways: he appointed artists and men of letters as ambassadors, and sometimes offered them as "gifts," as was the case with Leonardo, sent to Milan to the court of Ludovico Sforza, known as *il Moro* (1452–1508) in early 1482. Most artists of the time were not able to manage without prominent patrons, and Leonardo was not in a position to refuse the powerful Lorenzo. In any event, he had reason to be pleased with his lord's choice: Milan seemed to be the ideal place for realizing his numerous aspirations. Ludovico was officially only a regent, but in reality the uncontested tyrant of the duchy of Milan, a man tireless in his pursuit of power, who lived in a castle that looked like a fortress. At the same time, Ludovico planned to transform his city

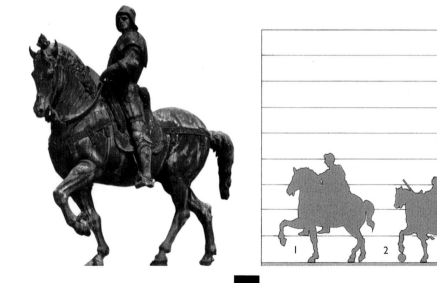

into a new Athens, surrounding himself with scholars and outstanding artists. While exercising absolute power over the duchy, he also promoted new techniques of irrigation, designed to increase the yield of the recently planted rice fields.

The Colossus

Eager to make a name for himself, Leonardo took on his first assignment: the creation of a gigantic equestrian statue of Ludovico's father, Francesco Sforza: the so-called colossus.

This project, which involved creating a 22 foot- (7 meter-) high statue on a rearing horse, and the ensuing insurmountable difficulties in casting the bronze, were to torment Leonardo for many years.

Ludovico, in the meantime, criticized and threatened the artist. Leonardo had a clay model built of the

3   4   5

colossus, but despite his best intentions, new interests drew him away from this ambitious project.

The Virgin of the Rocks

Ludovico assigned Leonardo a stipend of 500 ducats a year, but in 1483, Leonardo was able to accept a contract from the brothers of the Immaculate Conception for a painting to be displayed in their chapel in the church of San Francesco Grande.

Leonardo began work on a composition that came to be known as *The Virgin of the Rocks*. He was to make a second version ten years later: the first is now in Paris, while the second is in London.

Many familiar themes from Leonardo's works appear in the first painting, completed between 1483 and 1486: the close attention to natural elements, lighting effects, and the characters' gestures, which give the composition the power of a narrative.

Anatomy

Leonardo also created portraits, to which he brought a new intensity, as in the case of the *Lady with an Ermine*. However, painting was only one of many activities that filled his busy days in Milan. His insatiable curiosity was piqued by studies of anatomy, as well, which corresponded to the need he felt as a painter to represent the human figure in as precise a way as possible.

Using their knowledge of anatomy, Renaissance painters hoped to convey the effects of various conditions and situations on human figures: the effects of

Hands
In this painting, Leonardo conveys a sense of dialogue through gestures. The angel, behind the infant Jesus, points to Saint John the Baptist who, with hands joined in prayer, acknowledges the future redeemer. Jesus, in return, blesses the child who will one day announce his coming to the world.

Light
Notice Leonardo's remarkable attention to light in this painting. It comes from several different sources: one in front of the scene, and two weaker ones in the background.

intense effort, for example, which would entail specific reactions, positions, and facial expressions.

Science
Leonardo's passion in the most general sense was for science. His infinite curiosity found satisfaction in his friendship with the Franciscan monk Luca Pacioli, also at Sforza's court, a great popularizer of mathematics, which was a much-studied discipline at the time.

Following the conquest of Constantinople by the Turks in 1453, refugee scholars took with them to Italy precious manuscripts that broadened

DISSECTION
During the fifteenth century, the dissection of corpses took place in secret at first, then in an increasingly open manner.

then-current knowledge of algebra and geometry.

Pacioli calculated the volume of the horse Leonardo had yet to fuse and determined the precise quantity of bronze that would be needed. Because of his diverse interests, Leonardo has always been considered a "polyhedric" or many-sided genius. Still, one must not forget his aversion for cultural hierarchies: for the distinction between the liberal and the mechanical arts, for example. Leonardo believed that the value and dignity of painting were equal to those of philosophy and science. He was "the artist of science," because scientific research constituted the basis of his artistic endeavors.

SCIENTIFIC KNOWLEDGE
On the basis of numerous dissections, Leonardo created representations of the muscular and nervous system, arterial circulation, and the skeleton.

Anatomy
The modern science of anatomy was founded in the mid-sixteenth century by the Flemish Andreas Vesalius.

Consider the way he sought to represent reality: he did not merely imitate the *forms* of reality, but sought to determine the *causes and effects* of human life and nature in general. He strove to understand the phenomena of the natural world and to represent them in an exhaustive, creative manner.

Though Leonardo sometimes seemed to be "the practical man in search of a theory," he was always an artist who sought to go further, to capture that which was eluding him. Leonardo, it has been said, didn't seek: he found . . . .

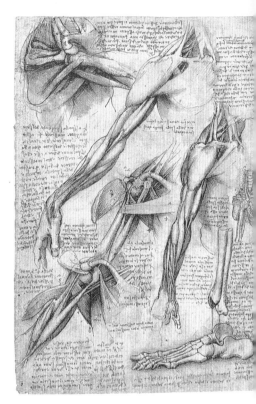

The Codices

Five years after his arrival in Milan, Leonardo created a written form for his many varied ideas and theoretical, practical, artistic, and technological discoveries. He took to compiling all his different types of notes and sketches in notebooks of various dimensions.

These notes today comprise Leonardo's *Codices*, some of which have been discovered in recent years, in which the scientist, the engineer, and the artist offer a series of "visual notes": an intriguing endeavor that combines allegories and technical revelations, fantastic forms and practical insights, in a rich texture of art and science, experimentation and philosophy.

Some of the drawings in the *Codices* represent surprising anticipations of modern and contemporary technology.

The "new city"

Leonardo was up to the exacting standards of Ludovico Sforza as an archi-

Anatomical and technical illustrations
On the left, an example of the accuracy with which Leonardo is capable of representing muscles and joints. On the right, a study on the table saw with mathematical calculations.

Movable type
The invention of modern typography by Johannes Gutenberg in 1439 represented a huge step forward in the spread of knowledge.

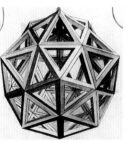

Luca Pacioli (1445–1514)
A Franciscan friar, his *Summa de arithmetica, geometria, proportioni et proportionalità* was critical for bringing mathematics to the public.

Polygons
Leonardo drew a series of polygons as illustrations for Luca Pacioli's treatise, *De divina proportione*.

tect and urban planner, as well. Leonardo's patron made his own original contributions as an organizer of festivities and theatrical presentations. He had a natural inclination for such artistic pursuits: his dynamic set designs and theatrical devices combined well with his passion for literature and music (he was a virtuoso performer), and with his taste for allegory.

But Ludovico was not concerned only with courtly life: he demanded from his architects innovative solutions for transforming the old medieval city into a modern ideal city. To this end, Donato Bramante, Francesco di Giorgio, and Antonio Amadeo drew up plans for churches, convents, and other buildings, while Leonardo set his hand to a series of urban planning projects. He envisioned a "new city," taking functionality as prime concern, but without neglecting the great variety of urban levels: from the highest and noblest to that of the sewers. Running water was important for hygienic reasons: in Leonardo's "new city," waterways were the prime arteries for both practical reasons and as a means for ensuring health.

Though he presented his plans in 1492, none of them was ever realized. Leonardo's ideas for city-planning (which have come down to us only in part) have nothing to do with the Renaissance tradition of the utopian city: they are "futuristic," but based on knowledge of the environment and

A NEW QUARTER
The plague of 1465 revealed the disastrous hygienic conditions of central Milan. Leonardo envisioned a quarter that for the first time would offer basic features for protecting public health.

Elevated roads
In his plans, Leonardo separated roads for wagons from roads for pedestrians, which ran under arcades and were protected from the rain.

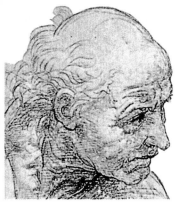

Donato Bramante
(1444–1514)
Educated at the court of Urbino, he lived in Milan starting in 1477, after which he worked as an architect in Rome.

A central plan
Renaissance architects were fascinated by geometry. Buildings with a central plan could be inscribed in a circle or in a square.

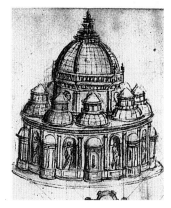

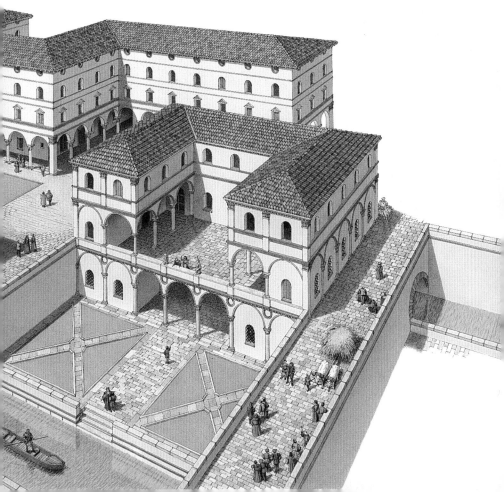

scientific rigor. Along with Bramante, Leonardo undertook research and planning for churches that revived the traditional central plan. Bramante was to continue this quest for classical values in his studies and in actual monuments, most notably in the latter part of his life, which he spent in Rome.

Santa Maria delle Grazie

In 1494, with the death of his nephew Gian Galeazzo, the legitimate heir to the duchy, Ludovico finally became the official, universally recognized duke of Milan. He was particularly interested in the Dominican church of Santa Maria delle Grazie, which would become in the last years of the fifteenth century the most "effervescent" workshop in the city.

Amadeo, Bramante, and Leonardo himself were involved in the work to expand, transform, and decorate the complex that Ludovico hoped would become the mausoleum for the Sforza family. Leonardo's assignment was to fresco the rear wall of the convent's refectory. Facing a wall on which a *Crucifixion* of Christ is depicted, Leonardo created an extraordinary and soon-to-be famous representation of *The Last Supper* of Christ and his disciples. Leonardo chose the moment in the Gospels when Jesus tells his followers that one of them will soon betray him. As one who had long studied human emotions and gestures, Leonardo once again concentrated on the attitudes of his characters. Each disciple, according to

The lantern and the apse
The lantern, composed of a gallery with 16 sides and 32 mullion windows, was the work of Giovanni Antonio Amadeo (1447–1522). Bramante supervised the work for the square-based apse beneath the lantern.

THE LAST SUPPER
Painted in oil and tempera, the work measures 346½" by 181" (4.6 by 8.8 meters). Intrinsically fragile, it has been restored, retouched, and even repainted several times.

his age and personality, reacts in a different manner to Jesus's terrible announcement, expressing his distress in his own unique way: looking at the painting is like reliving their emotions on

that Passover evening when Jesus established the sacrament of the Eucharist. The work was completed between 1495 and 1498. Barely a year later, Milan and its surrounding territories were invaded by the troops of King Louis XII of France. Ludovico Sforza fled to Germany, and French soldiers destroyed the colossal clay model of the equestrian statue that Leonardo had never cast, and never would cast. Along with his friend Luca Pacioli,

1

In the shadows, Judas (1) is the only disciple who does not express suffering: he, along with Jesus, is aware of the terrible secret. With his hands raised, the disciple Andrew (2) seems to want to drive something away. Philip (3) gathers his hands upon his breast. Matthew (4), with his arms stretched out toward Jesus, casts an unbelieving, desperate glance at the two apostles seated at the end of the table.

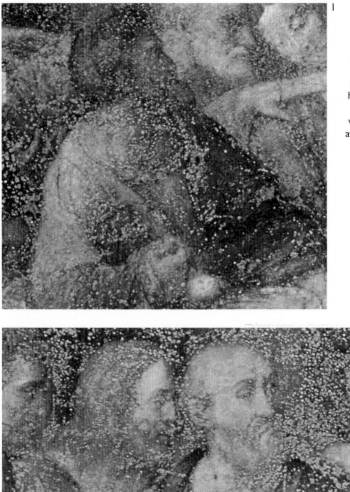

2

3

Leonardo fled Milan. After 17 years in the service of the Sforza family, he was forced to look for new patrons. It is likely that his first stop was Mantua, at the court of Isabella d'Este, the famous "muse" of the Italian Renaissance; he then planned defenses for the Venetian Republic against the threat of the Turkish invasion, at the same time drawing up plans for a bridge over the Bosphorous for the Sultan. He also settled in Piombino, in the service of Cesare Borgia (1475–1507), the son of Pope Adrian VI, who had created his own duchy through sheer brute force. In short, Leonardo "made a virtue of necessity," as he was fond of saying throughout his life.

4

MICHELANGELO AND LORENZO

In Florence, during Lorenzo the Magnificent's reign, a solitary young sculptor was just starting out. It is said that from his earliest years, Michelangelo "breathed" marble dust. He excelled in drawing but did not consider himself a painter.

In 1475, more or less when Leonardo da Vinci was about to leave Verrocchio's workshop and start his own career as an artist and scientist, the life of another genius of the High Renaissance began. Michelangelo Buonarroti was born on March 6, 1475. He, too, was Tuscan, from Caprese (near Arezzo). His father, Ludovico Buonarroti Simoni, was at the time *podestà* (or chief magistrate) of Chiusi and Caprese: this position was modest compared with those once held by members of his old Florentine family.

The family returned to Florence and sent their son to a wet nurse in Settignano, a small village of stonecutters about two miles from the city, where the Buonarrotis owned a farm.

Michelangelo's mother, Francesca di Neri, a distant relative of the Medicis, died when her son was barely six. Michelangelo's life with his father, a somber and discontented

Stonecutters' work
Stonecutters sawed slabs, polished capitals, and molded decorative elements.

In this small town, which had been home to generations of stonecutters and stone-masons, Michelangelo became familiar with the tools and techniques for working *pietra serena*.

Portraits in stone
Bust of Marietta Strozzi created in marble by Desiderio da Settignano (c. 1455).

MOLDINGS
A good stonecutter was able to create linear decorative elements (including frames and trimmings) that would join together perfectly.

Michelangelo's wet nurse
The daughter and wife of a stonecutter, she said that young Michelangelo drank marble powder along with her milk.

man, was not happy; he was sent to be educated to the humanist Francesco Galatea, who gave him a solid training in grammar and literature, the basis for the poetic sensibility that would emerge later in his long life. But the boy's greatest passion was for drawing.

When Michelangelo was thirteen, his friend Francesco Granacci (who was eight years older) brought him to the celebrated workshop of Domenico Ghirlandaio (1449–1494). As a teacher, Ghirlandaio had neither the patience nor the multifaceted talents of Verrocchio, but he probably was Florence's most fashionable painter of the moment. His great talent for depicting the forms and customs of civic life won him the name of the "chronicler" of Florence. When Michelangelo joined them, Ghirlandaio's workshop was frescoing a chapel in the church

Pen and ink
Pen and ink was the most common technique in the workshops. A study by Ghirlandaio of *The Betrothal of the Virgin*.

of Santa Maria Novella. *Ser* Ludovico was not happy with his son's choice of career, which he considered unworthy of the family. But Michelangelo, an apprentice like no other, was not required to pay for room and board (a highly unusual arrangement for the time), and was actually awarded a small stipend as a student and junior assistant. That helped to overcome his father's resistance. Michelangelo had apparently already learned to draw, perhaps from Granacci: his style was

Paints
Paints were sometimes spread onto paper, particularly for drawings created by scratching the pigment with metal points.

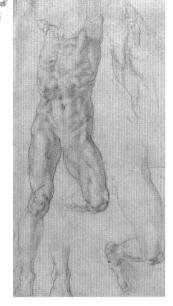

Charcoal
Charcoal's soft line made it ideal for studies and sketches. Michelangelo, *Portrait of Andrea Quaresi.*

Sanguine
Michelangelo often drew using red pencils (or sanguine), made from rust-colored clay. *Male Figure, 1508–1512.*

so new and personal that Ghirlandaio was astounded, and even somewhat envious of him. The two did not have an ideal relationship, and Ghirlandaio's influence on his pupil was practically nonexistent. Michelangelo, on his own, sought out his own teachers all over Florence: he made copies of the figures in Donatello's statues, in Giotto's frescoes in Santa Croce, and in Masaccio's frescoes in the Brancacci chapel of the Chiesa del Carmine. Michelangelo's first drawings showed an energy and a sense of intellectual independence that were quite rare for the workshops of the time.

Michelangelo worked by himself and insisted on executing his works on his own, from the first to the very last stroke. He was unable to adapt himself to the collaborative spirit that saw students and assistants making contributions to a master's work, particularly in the case of fresco cycles or other complex projects. Leonardo had done so under Verrocchio, but Michelangelo did not have this ability. The workshop cramped his spirit, and he perhaps already thought of art as the expression of an individual creative force.

Lorenzo the Magnificent

In contrast to the closed, fortified castle of Ludovico Sforza in Milan, the splendid Renaissance *palazzo* in Via Larga belonging to the Medici family fit in harmoniously with the rest of the city, and was similar to the dwellings of other rich Florentine merchant and banker families. The Medicis guided

Intensity of expression
In his cycle of frescoes for the Brancacci Chapel, Masaccio did not simply create realistic representations, in form and dimension, of human subjects and environments. He offered a profound interpretation of the variety of human emotion: the dignified, deeply felt gratitude of the woman receiving charity in the *Distribution of Alms and Death of Anania*; the pride and assurance of Peter in *Saint Peter Cures the Sick with his Own Shadow*.

The chapel
The Brancacci Chapel is in the Chiesa del Carmine in Florence.

The chapel
It was frescoed by
Benozzo Gozzoli
in 1459.

The courtyard
The entrance was
in Via Larga.

The *piano nobile*
Delegations were
received in great hall

the affairs of state from their *palazzo:* though they usually held no official public offices, their "counsels" were in fact orders, enforced by their faithful followers.

Lorenzo led the family from 1469 on. Kind and cultivated, he was known as "the Magnificent" because of his political ability, and because of his great love for culture and the arts. Lorenzo crafted a prudent foreign policy, forming alliances, loaning money to the great powers of the age, and "exporting" his best talents (as was the case with Leonardo) to promote the glory of Florence. The most illustrious

Medici festivities
This banquet took place in the courtyard of the Medici *palazzo* and was depicted in a miniature (1460) by Apollonio di Giovanni.

The Medici *palazzo*
It was designed and built between 1444 and 1459 by Michelozzo, a pupil of Brunelleschi. The inner facade opens onto an elegant courtyard, with a loggia marked by columns. The fortified wall on the garden side offered protection against popular uprisings.

intellectuals of the time lived in his *palazzo*, surrounded by his beloved collections of medals, cameos, and precious stones.

These great scholars included Marsilio Ficino, who translated Plato into Latin and founded the Platonic Academy; the poet Agnolo Poliziano, who lectured on Homer and Aristotle; and Pico della Mirandola, a man of prodigious learning with an unsurpassed memory.

The garden at San Marco
Lorenzo's sculpture collection was

displayed in the garden near the church of San Marco, where there had sprung up a sculpture school led by Bertoldo di Giovanni, who worked with Donatello. Michelangelo found the atmosphere in the garden much more stimulating than in the restricted, arduous world of the workshop. Lorenzo soon grew fond of him and invited him to join his household, as well as assimilate the foundations of his style. Michelangelo lived in Via Larga until 1492, the year of Lorenzo's death, and when Michelangelo completed what he considered the finest of his early works: the bas-relief depicting *The Battle of the Centaurs*. The motif was taken from an episode of the *Metamorphoses* by the Latin poet Ovid: the battle between centaurs, mythological creatures with the head and torso of a man and the body of a horse, and a peaceful people from Thessaly, Greece.

THE GARDEN AT SAN MARCO
The garden was a meeting place for artists, writers, and philosophers. Lorenzo's ancient statues were displayed inside a brick arcade, where artists studied and copied them. It was in this environment that Michelangelo's love for sculpture, literature, and humanistic thought was born. Lorenzo apparently first took note of the young artist after seeing the head of a fawn he had sculpted in marble, inspired by an ancient statue.

Centaurs
The sense of space is created by a tangle of bodies, from the center of which emerges the figure of a young man with his arm raised at an angle.

48

RAPHAEL IN URBINO

Duke Federico brought splendor to the court of Urbino. Piero della Francesca, Francesco di Giorgio, and Bramante combined art, experiments in perspective, and mathematics. Raphael trained and began his quest for perfection in painting here.

While England, France, and Spain were becoming increasingly centralized and powerful nations, fifteenth-century Italy remained divided into small- and medium-sized states. In the climate of peace and stability that reigned in the second half of the century, the noble courts, great families, and various economic organizations of the different regions promoted grand works of art and cultural activities. Florence and Milan were not alone in this regard: Mantova and Rimini also hosted cultivated, sumptuous, and refined courts. The Republic of Venice was the homeland of great painters—Giovanni Bellini, above all—whose explorations of light and color gave rise to extraordinary works. At the beginning of the sixteenth century, the papal court reinvigorated Rome, which became the peninsula's new artistic capital. In this general landscape, a small court of

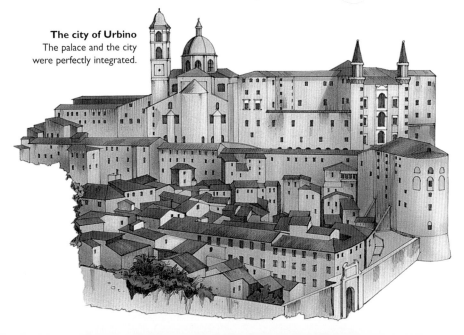

The city of Urbino
The palace and the city were perfectly integrated.

The Flagellation
Dating from 1460, this work by Piero della Francesca testifies to his mastery of perspective. The young man in the red tunic is Federico's half-brother, Oddantonio, with the conspirators who murdered him in 1444.

central Italy—the court of Urbino— quickly rose to prominence, and just as quickly declined.

Its destiny was tied to that of its duke, Federico da Montefeltro. A renowned mercenary captain, he became feudal lord of Urbino by the grace of Pope Sixtus IV. He was an extremely cultivated man, a patron and collector of artworks, and the owner of a library with more than 1100 volumes on the science and art of war. The Tuscan painter Piero della Francesca created some of his most celebrated works in Urbino. Piero was one of the most important painters of the Renaissance, though his lack of worldliness and the complexity of his "scientific" ideas make him unknown to most art lovers, and loved by only a few. *The Flagellation* is one work by Piero directly related to Urbino, for it tells the story of Federico's young half-brother.

Urbino's palace
Federico was in many respects similar to Lorenzo the Magnificent, though his great palace in Urbino was dramatically different from the Medici residence in Florence's Via Larga. The single elements of the Urbino palace, in their forms and dimensions, reflect the principles of balance, symmetry,

and harmony characteristic of Renaissance architecture.

But the extreme complexity and consequent "fragmentary" nature of the enormous complex also represent an anomaly in Italian Renaissance architecture. An unequivocal representation of Federico's ambition, the palace was inserted into the already existing city center, radically changing its aspect: was it a palace in the form of a city, or a city in the form of a palace? Along with Luciano Laurana, Francesco di Giorgio Martini, the great architect from Siena, supervised the building site, which remained open for 30 years, from 1455 to 1485. Still, starting in the 1470s, with Piero's arrival, the palace had become a meeting place for such Italian and foreign painters, including the Flemish painter Giusto di Gand, and the Spaniard Pedro Berruguete, who decorated the most famous area of the palace: Federico's intimate *studiolo*.

Raphael's earliest years

On April 6, 1483—a year after the death of Duke Federico—Raphael was born in the refined city of Urbino. He was a child of the arts: his father,

Federico da Montefeltro's Studiolo
Walls covered in wood mosaic create the illusion of furnishings and architectural elements.

THE CITY IN THE FORM OF A PALACE
Urbino and its palace weren't a finished work, but an assemblage of different parts set upon varied geometric levels.

Respect for the past
In addition to the façade, which houses the ducal apartments, numerous wings spread out harmoniously around a hanging garden and three courtyards. The palace was set into the city in a way that respected the pre-existing urban structure, which dated back to Roman times.

The function of the portrait *Federico da Montefeltro*, a portrait by Pedro Berruguete. In the fifteenth century, the portrait had an obvious symbolic function. Noblemen preferred to be depicted with dogs and falcons, which evoked hunting, an aristo-cratic pastime; with leopards, which were noble and strong beasts (like noble-men themselves); with books, because true nobility could not neglect learning; and in armor, since many lords had come to power through the use of arms.

 Giovanni di Sante di Pietro (called "Santi" or "Sanzio"), was a painter at the ducal court, then led by Federico's son, Guidobaldo, and Elisabetta Gonzaga, Guidobaldo's wife.

Raphael's father was considered a mediocre poet and painter, but the fact that Raphael was the son of an artist made his position very different from that of Michelangelo and Leonardo, who needed to overcome their fathers' resistance before setting off to the workshop to learn their art. Raphael's first teacher was his father, through whom he also gained access to the works of Melozzo da Forlì, Luca della Robbia, Van Eyck, Giusto di Gand,

Raphael or Perugino?
This *Crucifixion* from 1503 was signed by Raphael, though the manner is Perugino's. The master and pupil influenced each other reciprocally, though it was Perugino who eventually conformed to Raphael's style.

Leonardo, and Perugino. Just before dying in 1494, his father entrusted Raphael to Perugino's workshop. Raphael also lost his mother, Magia di Battista, but he was brought up attentively and with love in the court of Urbino. An apprentice in Perugia's most important workshop, Raphael soon revealed himself to be a child prodigy.

Perugino's workshop
Pietro Vannucci, known as Perugino (c. 1445–1523) was the greatest representative of the Umbrian school: a style of painting characterized by delicacy, the strong influence of Piero della Francesca's rigorous use of perspective, and a great attentiveness to nature learned from Verrocchio.

The destinies of the three giants of the High Renaissance came together in this episode: at the end of the 1460s, when Leonardo entered Verrocchio's workshop, he met Perugino, who was slightly older and busy completing his apprenticeship.

Perugino gave his pupils great freedom to develop their skills: his assistants contributed to paintings commissioned from the master, and he sometimes merely supervised their work. As a result, Raphael matured quite rapidly as an artist. The *Crucifixion* of 1503 confirmed the ties

between Perugino and Raphael, but *The Betrothal of the Virgin,* barely a year later, gave proof of the pupil's full autonomy. The three principal figures—the High Priest, Mary, and Joseph—are set within a composition with a single center, like Bramante and Leonardo's work, in which the delicate gestures of the three protagonists create additional interrelations among them. A comparison of *The Betrothal* to Perugino's fresco for the Sistine Chapel, the *Consegna delle chiavi* (painted 15 years earlier) shows analogies, but also important differences. In Perugino's painting the figures crowd together in several distinct groupings,

without a strong, organic relationship between the figures and the architectural elements. In Raphael's work, the composition is built on geometric relationships, on precise proportions among the component parts. Its "lesson" is that of Piero della Francesca: beauty corresponds with geometric order.

An optimist, by nature sweet and kind, Raphael was also curious and ambitious. He had nothing more to learn in Perugia; the court of Urbino was declining rapidly; and so he looked to the city that was still (for a short while longer) the most fascinating home for an artist: Florence.

THE FLORENTINE REPUBLIC

It was the last, brief moment of artistic splendor in Florence: Savanarola and Machiavelli took part in political struggles, Leonardo worked in the city for two years, and Michelangelo's *David* showed the city's pride. And then there was Raphael.

In 1492, following Lorenzo de' Medici's death, Michelangelo was forced to return to his father's house. Lorenzo's death represented a severe blow for Michelangelo and for Florence; it also brought about the demise of the politics of "equilibrium" among the various Italian states, with disastrous consequences that were felt all too soon. Two years later, with the encouragement of Ludovico il Moro, Charles VIII of France and his troops descended upon the Italian peninsula, intent

SAN MARCO
Life in this Dominican convent, where Savanarola was abbot, was marked by the rhythm of prayer, study, and preaching to the faithful.

upon conquering the Kingdom of Naples.

Thus began 65 years of war.

Lorenzo's son, Piero de' Medici, proved so weak when confronted with the arrogance of the invaders that the Florentines, led by the Dominican friar Girolamo Savanarola, overturned the Medicis and set up a theocratic republic. It was dominated on the one hand by Savanarola's followers (called *Piagnoni* or "moaners" because of their austerity), and on the other by the local aristocracy. Even Michelangelo, who had been so strongly influenced by neoplatonic philosophy, was fascinated by the friar, who delivered thunderous sermons condemning the corruption of the Roman curia and of the Borgia pope, Alexander VI, all the while stirring up passionate hatred.

Before the founding of the republic, Michelangelo's precarious

THE CONVENT
The complex consisted of a church, which led to the cloister; of cells, which had been decorated by Beato Angelico; of a large library; and of a guesthouse for pilgrims.

Girolamo Savanarola
A portrait by Fra Bartolomeo, from the early sixteenth century.

personal and political situation had led him to leave Florence for Venice and Bologna, where he was able to find work. It was probably then that he began writing his first poems and studying intently the vernacular works of his beloved Dante and Petrarch. Michelangelo returned to Florence in 1495, but left for Rome and the household of Cardinal Riario in 1496. He was preceded by the fame of his *Sleeping Cupid*—which had been "aged" and sold as an ancient statue.

Indeed, it was classical sculpture (including the *Belvedere torso*) that inspired Michelangelo's most famous statues: the *Bacchus* in the Bargello, and the *Pietà,* commissioned by Charles VIII's ambassador, possibly as a funerary decoration. When working on the *Pietà,* Michelangelo went to Carrara for the first time, to pick out his own marble.

The *David*

Michelangelo returned to Florence in 1501. Savanarola had been excommu-

A RECURRING SUBJECT
David, who defeated the giant Goliath, was portrayed and reinterpreted by many Renaissance artists.

Hercules as David
The pose of this bronze miniature, possibly by Bertoldo, resembles Michelangelo's *David.*

Introspective
The ideal beauty, inspired by the classical world, of Donatello's *David* (1430–1433).

Charles VIII
The entry of the French king into Florence in a painting by Francesco Granacci.

Michelangelo's David
The most famous and admired *David* in all the world.

nicated by the pope (who had also threatened to interdict the government) and burned alive in *Piazza della Signoria.* The city was in the hands of a merchant oligarchy.

From an artistic point of view, Florence was still the most advanced city of Italy (and of the western world), though it would remain so for only a few years.

The *gonfaloniere* Pier Soderini, to promote the Florentine republic, called back to the city all the artists who had left, including Leonardo. In 1500, he was received in his homeland with the greatest honors.

Michelangelo had only a few commissions, but the new government gave him an immense block of marble which had been clumsily carved by Agostino di Duccio 40 years earlier. Michelangelo proceeded to "extract" a colossal *David,* who embodied the humanistic theme of the hero. This *David,* though, is neither a triumphant hero boldly displaying the symbol of his victory, nor a warrior locked in battle: his body is tense and compressed, captured in the instant that precedes battle, ready to release its tension with a single gesture. He is not yet in movement: the energy is concentrated in the muscles of his neck, which twist his head about violently.

An unresolved conflict

Soderini's various commissions, unprecedented since ancient times, and whose goal was the exaltation of civic, secular, and political values, came to focus on a unique and magnificent undertaking. With typically Florentine cunning and calculation, Soderini invited both Leonardo and Michelangelo to decorate the *sala del Maggior Consiglio* in the *palazzo della Signoria.* Though not exactly rivals, the two artists were in many ways at odds. Leonardo, the older man, sculpted in bronze, not marble. He was a celebrated artist and a friend of powerful lords who had returned to Florence to take his place at the summit of the artistic world. Michelangelo, only 28 years old, was a rising star, a reserved man who preferred to work in secret, without showing his work to anyone. The two may even have had a public falling out, with the younger, less famous Michelangelo taunting his elder for not having finished the Sforza equestrian statue—which remained a thorn in Leonardo's side.

Soderini commissioned two frescoes depicting victorious battles from Florence's military history.

Leonardo was assigned *The Battle of Anghiari,* fought against the Milanese in 1440, while Michelangelo

The *David*'s path
The *David* advanced slowly in the narrow streets from Michelangelo's studio (behind the *Duomo*), its head sometimes towering above the roofs.

Choosing a setting for the *David* was an arduous task. It was finally placed in front of the *palazzo della Signoria*, though *piazza del Duomo* was also considered.

Leonardo's views
He had proposed that *David* be placed in the *loggia dell'Orcagna*. Michelangelo took offense.

Transporting the *David*
Forty men spent four days pulling the *David* on greased rollers.

Protecting the *David*
The statue was strapped into a wooden framework using a system of pulleys and counterpoises.

was assigned *The Battle of Cascina*, fought against Pisa in 1354.

For various reasons—because of Leonardo's poor technical choices, and also because of Julius II's grandiose plans for Rome, which involved Michelangelo—both artists abandoned their work, and their preparatory drawings were eventually lost. Michelangelo's drawing was destroyed because it was *too* admired: it was copied numerous times, divided up,

Its function
It was the seat of political power in the Florentine republic.

The Palazzo Vecchio
It was built starting in 1299 using plans by the architect Arnolfo di Cambio (c. 1245–c. 1308).

and distributed to various courts. Leonardo's depiction of the battle is known only thanks to his beautiful preparatory drawings and the many copies of the painting, including a drawing by the Flemish painter, Pieter Paul Rubens (1577–1640).

A pivotal year: 1504

Raphael's arrival in Florence in 1504 brought together the three greatest geniuses of the High Renaissance.

Raphael was 21 years old and was aware of the battle drawings and their reputation. He made a presentation to Soderini, but the *gonfaloniere* did not receive him warmly. Raphael received no public commissions in Florence, but he had outgrown Umbria, and had numerous opportunities to take an active part in the Tuscan city's artistic life: in addition to Leonardo and Michelangelo, such fine painters as Ridolfo del Ghirlandaio (1483–1561) and fra' Bartolomeo (1475–1517) lived and worked in Florence. Raphael observed and learned—from Leonardo, about the blending of colors and the fusion of figures into space; from Michelangelo, about the dynamic potential of drawing and the development of forms using the geometry of the spiral and the pyramid.

During the years he was in Florence and Urbino, Raphael completed his first series of Madonnas: the *Madonna del Granduca;* the *Madonna del Cardellino;* and the *Belle Jardinère.* He also created portraits of members of the Florentine merchant aristocracy, including a portrait in the manner of Leonardo of the prosperous Agnolo Doni.

Leonardo's drawings
Leonardo's many beautiful preparatory drawings are all that remain of his *Battle of Anghiari,* and allow us to understand how the painting might have looked. The warrior's heads and the rearing horses suggest the ferocity of the battle between the Florentines and the Milanese, which took place near Arezzo.

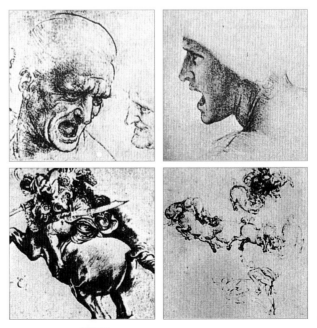

The warming pans
They were used to heat the walls, so the wax would spread more easily.

The screws
They had a double threading, to the right and to the left, for raising and lowering the scaffolding.

A DOUBLE BATTLE
Though the Florentines had won at Anghiari, Leonardo lost his battle with encaustic. His misinterpretation of ancient texts on the subject and use of warming pans to heat the walls caused the colors to dissolve.

A famous copy
Rubens copied the central portion of the *Battle of Anghiari*.

The scaffolding
Leonardo invented a special type of scaffolding for the occasion: using a special type of screw, workers were able to raise and lower it as needed.

Michelangelo, too, after his disappointing trip to Rome, worked for the Doni family.

Julius II had asked Michelangelo to draw up plans for his tomb, but like many powerful men, he was capricious, and Michelangelo grew tired of the constant delays. He returned to Florence and agreed to create for the Doni family a painting of the Sacred Family with young Saint John (the *Tondo Doni*), in which he expressed the shift of an age, from the pagan era to the Judeo-Christian world.

Set behind a small embankment, the group of male nudes in the background represent the pagan world, prior to Moses. In the foreground, the Madonna, who turns slightly to receive the Christ child from Saint Joseph, symbolizes the Christian world, sanctified by grace. In the middle ground, the young Saint John the Baptist leans against the wall and looks towards the Sacred Family: he alone is conscious of Truth. The colors chosen by Michelangelo are bright, cold, and juxtaposed with a certain severity. The slight *chiaroscuro* (variation of light and shade) creates the effect of marble.

The *Tondo Doni*
Completed in 1506, the *Tondo Doni* is the only painting by Michelangelo that is not a fresco.

In the meantime, Leonardo had started working on the portrait of a lady with a mysterious smile and an intense glance. It was *La Gioconda (Mona Lisa)*, the famous painting on which the artist was to work right up until his death. At the same time, he continued his studies of engineering, drawing up plans for a navigable canal (never realized) which, fed by rivers descending from the Apennine mountains, would have linked Florence and Pisa.

The happy coincidence that had brought the three geniuses together in Florence did not last long: in 1506, Leonardo returned to Milan and Michelangelo was called back to Rome, where Raphael was to follow in

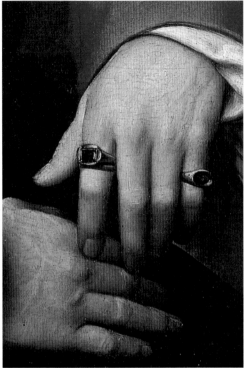

Agnolo Doni
A portrait of Agnolo Doni by
Raphael (1506). Raphael brought
new dimensions to the secular
portrait, as well as to sacred
paintings.

In the manner of Leonardo
Raphael admired Michelangelo
but learned much more from
Leonardo. The close up of Agnolo
Doni's hands reminds us of the
grace of the *Mona Lisa*.

1508. The papal court thus replaced
Florence as the center of the artistic
world.

In any event, the Florentine republic lasted only a few more years. In
1512, the Medicis returned to power,
no thanks to their own troops or to the
will of the Florentine people: it was the
Spanish army that allowed Giovanni
and Giuliano, the sons of Lorenzo the
Magnificent, to take power. Curtailing
its ambitions, the city of Florence
became a pawn in the Spanish political
scene.

LEONARDO IN THE NORTH

The lords of Florence pursued him, while the French governor demanded his presence in Milan: Leonardo created an international incident. In the end, the French kingdom of François I became his home.

The *gonfaloniere* of the Florentine Republic, Pier Soderini, was unhappy with the way things were turning out in the Sala del Maggior Consiglio, where he had intended to pit the painters Michelangelo and Leonardo against each other. Pope Julius II was pursuing Michelangelo, who divided his time between Rome and Florence; and Leonardo, too, was sought after by distant, powerful patrons. Louis XII of France personally demanded that Leonardo be released from his contract for the unhappy *Battle of Anghiari* so that he might join the service of duke Charles of Amboise, the French governor of Milan. The French were interested more in Leonardo's scientific abilities than in his artistic skills.

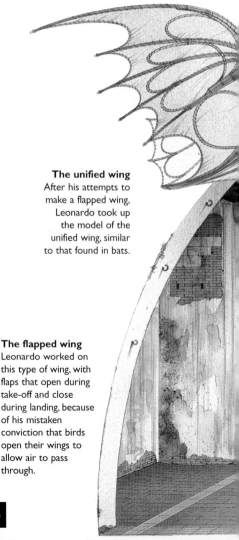

The unified wing
After his attempts to make a flapped wing, Leonardo took up the model of the unified wing, similar to that found in bats.

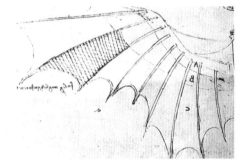

The flapped wing
Leonardo worked on this type of wing, with flaps that open during take-off and close during landing, because of his mistaken conviction that birds open their wings to allow air to pass through.

FLIGHT

Taking the flight of birds as his point of departure, Leonardo sought to realize his most fantastic invention: the flying machine. He designed a type of helicopter with an articulated, spring-driven wing.

Gliding

Leonardo was captivated by the idea of gliding—perhaps the only type of flight he might actually have achieved.

FILLING THE LOCK

The boat that has entered the lock must wait for the water from the upper level to fill up the basin to proceed to the exit level.

LOCKS

Leonardo can be considered the inventor of many hydraulic devices: in particular of locks, which control the level of water in canals and allow ships to proceed despite large differences in level.

Waterways

Waterways were extremely important: boats were more practical and economical than transport on wheels. Furthermore, most roads were in very poor shape.

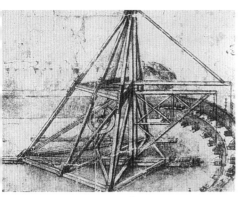

Improvements through machines
A design for a large excavator, with the power to proceed much more quickly than teams of workers with hoes and shovels.

In 1506, Leonardo left Florence, as we have already seen, returning there only briefly to deal with issues involving his uncle Francesco's estate.

The court of Milan was no longer filled with pomp and luxury, as it had been in the Moor's time: the French were in a constant state of alert against the maneuvers of Pope Julius II, who sought to drive them from Italy. Still, Milan remained a haven for artists and scholars.

Leonardo's second Milanese sojourn

Leonardo, surrounded by old and new apprentices, took up his favorite studies: perspective, the proportions of the human body, optics, hydraulics, aerostatics (the science of ballooning), and thermology. He "slipped," in a manner of speaking, in his second major undertaking as a sculptor because he failed to go beyond the preparatory drawings for the equestrian monument of marshall Gian Giacomo Trivulzio (who had supported the Moor's overthrow): once again, Leonardo had attempted to represent a knight on a rearing horse.

He took solace in hydraulics, searching for a way to make the Martesana canal, from Milan to Lake Como, navigable via a system of locks. The project was completed in 1509: though not quite the system Leonardo had envisioned, it allowed him to obtain concrete rewards from Louis XII, including a regular salary.

La Gioconda

The king, however, encouraged Leonardo not to neglect his artistic pursuits, and he started work on his *Bacchus, Saint Anne,* and other paintings in which the hand of his assistants can be clearly discerned. He also continued to work—alone and with loving attention—on *La Gioconda,* the painting he had brought with him from Florence. With this work, Leonardo created a kind of model for the portrait, one that would have great success throughout the ages: the naturalness and harmony of *La Gioconda* have no precedents in Renaissance painting.

His last travels

In the meantime, events unfolding in Milan were setting a new course for Leonardo's life. In 1511 his protector, Charles of Amboise, died; at the same time, the league of Italian states created by Julius II (with the help of Spain) drove the French out of Lombardy. Milan welcomed a new duke: Massimiliano Sforza, the son of Ludovico il Moro.

The new Sforza administration was inclined to mistrust those who had served the French, and they made no exception for Leonardo. He withdrew to Vaprio d'Adda, to the home of the nobleman Gerolamo Melzi, the father of Leonardo's beloved pupil Francesco. Discouraged and disappointed, Leonardo found new hope in the

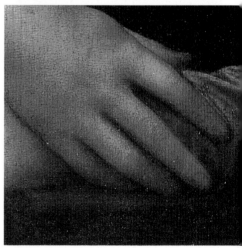

La Gioconda (Mona Lisa)
With an enigmatic smile and an intense glance, a woman is pictured in a landscape that fades away to the horizon and has in her delicate hands an instrument of seduction. The optical effects created by the refraction of light in the air give a sense of depth, thanks to the soft definition of objects—a technique known as "aerial perspective."

CHAMBORD
Between 1519 and 1550,
François I created on the banks
of the Loire River a residence
that remains the epitome of
French Renaissance splendor.
The main body is square, topped
by spires, towers, gables,
and cupolas.

election of the new pope: his friend, Cardinal Giovanni de' Medici, who took the name Leo X. In 1513 Leonardo, along with Francesco Melzi and other pupils, set out for Rome along with many other artists.

Leonardo hoped that Leo X would offer him the opportunities that Leo's father, Lorenzo the Magnificent, had denied him 33 years earlier, and this hope was fulfilled. He was assigned to work on the port of Civitavecchia and to reclaim the Pontine Marshes. At the same time, he plunged into studies of the classical world and of mythology (the Belvedere *Ariadne*), wrote descriptions of Roman ruins, painted, designed machines, invented costumes, dreamed of squaring the circle,

Leonardo's mark
Leonardo's hand can be seen in the criss-crossing plan of the halls, in the play of multiple forms on the roof, and in the great spiral staircase located in the right wing of the castle.

and created "robots" and geometrical games that he considered works of art, and not mere distractions. But he also went through periods of crisis and suffering: he quarreled with his expert machinist and was outraged by his rival Michelangelo's great success with the Sistine Chapel frescoes, so far removed from his own idea of painting.

At the Amboise court
In 1515, King Louis XII of France died and was succeeded by the young François I. Refined, elegant, a lady's man, and a passionate participant in hunts, jousts, and tournaments, François was obsessed by a single idea: crossing the Alps and invading Italy,

the only country (in his view) where "great and truly excellent things (were) achieved." He was most likely referring to Italy's artists and new culture, whose most prestigious representative was Leonardo. In 1517, the elderly master moved with his beloved Melzi to the Amboise court, on the banks of the Loire, where he was assigned the princely residence of Cloux and the title of painter, engineer, and architect of the realm, with an annual salary of ten thousand *scudi*.

The French court became a refined center of cultural relations in which he was the undisputed leader. He once again took part in theatrical production, re-creating some of his most fantastic devices, including the "mechanical lion." Though suffering from a kind of paralysis in his arm, he drew up plans for the new city of Romorantin. "Romolontino," as Leonardo himself called it, was never built, though François I used some of Leonardo's designs for his residence at Chambord.

In early 1519, Leonardo's health worsened and he died on May 2. Legend has it that François I rushed to his bedside, as if bidding farewell to his own father; Leonardo left all his manuscripts to Melzi, and *La Gioconda* watched Leonardo's passing with the smile that won him fame forever.

Self-portrait
The portrait dates from 1512, when Leonardo was 60, but he looks much older.

Amboise
Leonardo spent the last years of his life in Cloux, the royal residence.

ROBOTS
Leonardo was always passionately interested in robots. The one he created for François I boasted a spectacular effect: when opened using a mechanical device, it produced a shower of *fleurs de lis* (white lilies), the symbol of the French kingdom.

PAPAL ROME

The years of the Italian wars saw extraordinary achievements in politics, urban planning, and the arts in Rome. The Vatican became the peninsula's most important court and center of artistic patronage.

At the start of the sixteenth century, the Italian peninsula seemed to be a chessboard on which the great European nations were playing out their power game. Among the Italian states, only Venice and the Papal States retained some degree of autonomy and influence on the international scene. In Rome, Giuliano della Rovere had ascended to the throne of Saint Peter with the name Julius II (1503–1513), and proceeded to devise an elaborate plan whose goal was to give the head of the Catholic Church the greatest worldly power. He envisioned a kind of universal papacy, and dreamed of a warrior-pope with an iron will, who would behave just like any other prince

Julius II
The warrior-pope in his late 60s, as painted by Raphael. After many terrible years of war and religious disputes, Julius II appeared weak and tired.

of his times: waging war, surrounding himself with artists and intellectuals, and commissioning works of art. Julius called to his court the greatest artists of the times, to restore the image of Rome as the "eternal city" and center of the Christian world, and also to enhance the dignity and prestige of his own papacy.

Bramante, Michelangelo, and Raphael were all witnesses to and leaders of this cultural program, which seemed to its contemporaries to be the perfect realization of humanistic ideals.

Rome as "workshop"

Julius II saw Rome as the center of the world, the solemn continuation of the ancient imperial city, whose splendid ruins still endured. Since the early

Bramante
The *Tempietto* of San Pietro in Montorio, completed in the first decade of the sixteenth century, is a symbol of the Renaissance.

NEW ROME
Julius II assigned to Bramante the task of renewing the Roman cityscape by uniting the Vatican citadel with the different neighborhoods on both banks of the Tiber, setting the Vatican at the very center of Rome.

fifteenth century, artists and scholars had been studying the monuments of classical Rome, and it was from this new attention to the ancient world that Renaissance culture was born.

The renewed appeal of classical art had brought Donato Bramante to Rome from Milan in 1499, almost as if he had sensed the imminent downfall of his patron, Ludovico il Moro. In the eternal city he dedicated himself to rigorous, almost dogged studies of historic monuments, from which he drew an extraordinary variety of architectural images to emulate in his own works. His extensive efforts to recover the historic legacy of Rome coincided with Julius II's interests, and the pope asked Bramante to undertake an ambitious program of urban renewal, designed to transform Rome into the capital of the Christian world.

One of Bramante's creations was a long *cortile* (courtyard) between the Vatican palace and the Belvedere villa, designed to display the pope's collection of ancient sculpture, the finest that was known at the time. Bramante's innovation lay in the fact that this was a genuine open-air museum, in which each statue was set in a specific place—and not merely a display of art works in "random" spaces, as had been the case in the Medici's garden at San Marco.

The first statue displayed was the *Belvedere Apollo* (from the second century of the common era), which had been discovered a few years earlier in a courtyard belonging to the pope him-

The *Belvedere Torso*
This work by the Athenian sculptor Apollonius (from the first century before the common era) was discovered in the early fifteenth century.

Ruins
The remains of
an ionic colonnade,
possibly from a
temple dedicated
to Saturn.

self. In 1506, the *Laocoön* was found on a Roman estate and immediately purchased by the pope.

Bramante also drew up the plans for the new Saint Peter's Basilica. Inspired by the grandiose ideas of Bramante, who felt he was taking up where the ancients had left off, Julius II had the old basilica destroyed to make room for a new church that would be a symbol of the Church Triumphant and a

STUDY AND IMITATION

From the early fifteenth century on, Rome, with its vast array of ancient monuments, was visited by countless artists. Even Brunelleschi and Donatello traveled to Rome from Florence, in 1402 and 1404.

mausoleum for the first pope (Saint Peter) and his successors. Julius was not unmindful of himself, either. An ambitious man, he thought of a fitting place for his own tomb: when God called him, his body would lie in a grandiose monument composed of numerous statues, set in the center of Saint Peter's Basilica.

Julius II and Michelangelo

In the pope's view, only one artist was worthy of creating his tomb: the sculptor of Florence's *David*, Michelangelo Buonarrotti. When he left for Rome,

Michelangelo abandoned his work on the preliminary drawings for the *Battle of Cascina*. Michelangelo and the pope were to have a stormy relationship: Julius II was an authoritarian and rigid man, and Michelangelo was intransigent and highstrung. The artist spent eight months at Carrara choosing marble for Julius's tomb, only to see the commission taken away from him when the pope turned his attention to the new Saint Peter's. Disappointed and embittered, Michelangelo returned to Florence after turning down another commission from Julius II: to paint the ceiling of the Sistine Chapel.

The pope had his cavalry follow Michelangelo, and he also wrote an official letter—friendly in tone, but threatening in substance—to Pier Soderini,

The discovery of *Laocoön*
Michelangelo had been appointed superintendent of antiquities by the pope in early 1506. In this guise, he visited the site where the *Laocoön* had been found: a marble copy from the first century of the common era of a Hellenistic bronze statue.

the *gonfaloniere* of the Florentine republic, demanding that Michelangelo be returned to his court. Urged on by the Florentine government (who preferred to avoid a diplomatic incident), Michelangelo went to Bologna to make his peace with the pope.

Bologna had been the warrior-pope's latest military conquest and he wished to commemorate his victory with a work by Michelangelo. Julius II envisioned a bronze statue of himself placed in the facade of San Petronio, Bologna's cathedral. Michelangelo returned to Rome in 1508 and agreed to the pope's request—provided he also be allowed to resume work on the marble he had picked out for Julius's tomb. Still, the tomb was to torment Michelangelo almost until the end of his days.

THE APUAN HILLS
In Carrara, Michelangelo personally chose the marble for Julius II's tomb, and also supervised the quarrymen's work.

The finished tomb
The final version of the tomb, from 1545, was far simpler than the original plans, which called for 40 statues.

Moses
Placed in the central niche of the lower portion, the *Moses* anchors the entire composition. It is the only statue in the monument positively attributed to Michelangelo.

The slaves
The four marble statues created by Michelangelo for the pope's tomb are known as "slaves" or "prisoners" because they seem to be imprisoned by the marble.

THE SISTINE CHAPEL

Michelangelo agreed to fresco the ceiling of the Sistine Chapel. He considered himself more a sculptor than a painter. Despite his difficult relations with the pope, he created almost entirely on his own a work of grandiose scope.

The Sistine Chapel was the pope's private chapel, where he, his cardinals, and Rome's most illustrious visitors attended mass. Located in the heart of the Vatican, it had a special importance for Julius II: it was his uncle, Sixtus IV of the Della Rovere family, who had had the chapel built between 1475 and 1480, replacing an earlier structure. Sixtus IV asked that the chapel have the same dimensions attributed in the Bible to Solomon's Temple in Jerusalem: 132 by 44 feet (40.25 by 13.41 meters). From the outside, it resembled a small, fortified outpost of the papal palace.

To decorate the chapel, Sixtus summoned the most illustrious painters of the late fifteenth-century Florentine and Umbrian schools: many, including Botticelli and Perugino, had trained in Verrocchio's Florentine workshop during the time of Leonardo's apprenticeship.

The decoration for the Sistine Chapel depicted pairs of episodes in the lives of Moses and Christ, accompanied by an arcade with portraits of the very first popes. It was without doubt the most important pictorial undertaking of the late fifteenth century. As for the ceiling, Sixtus IV had asked that it be painted to resemble a starry sky, a common practice at that time. However, his nephew, Julius II, asked Michelangelo repeatedly to decorate the ceiling with figures of the twelve apostles.

A PAPAL VISIT
Julius II was pope from 1503 to 1513. He was a strong-willed man, both spiritual and military leader of the Church. He gave Michelangelo creative freedom but kept a close eye on his work, bursting into the Sistine workshop at the earliest opportunity.

The scaffolding
Bramante had envisioned a suspended walkway for the chapel. Michelangelo used existing holes in the walls for support.

Michelangelo was quick to modify Julius's plans for the decoration. While he dared not contradict the pope, and while he kept in mind the teachings of Rome's leading theologians, he asserted a truly

THE "CARTOONS"
All frescoes started as "cartoons," full-scale drawings of the images to be painted on the walls. The cartoons were cut up to correspond to the area to be painted on a particular day.

The *arriccio*
The surface was prepared by an assistant, who lay a preliminary layer, about an inch (2 cm) thick, of lime and volcanic dust.

Snapping the string
Two assistants, using a string covered with pigment, marked the portion of the wall to be frescoed.

The perforated cartoon
The drawing was perforated in several areas. The perforations were used to transfer the drawing to the plaster.

THE GIORNATA

After the *intonachino* (a second layer of plaster) was laid, it dried to produce calcium carbonate, which helped stabilize the colors. The painter needed to work quickly: the area of plaster that one could paint in the few hours before it dried was called the *giornata,* or day's work. First the perforated cartoon was placed against the ceiling; with a technique called "pouncing," the outlines of the figures were transferred to the wall. Finally, the artist began to paint.

Paints

Assistants ground and mixed paints. Michelangelo took care to use those most suited for frescoing.

revolutionary degree of artistic dignity and autonomy.

Even more remarkable was Michelangelo's ambition: to fresco an area covering nearly a thousand square meters by himself.

Michelangelo started the preliminary drawings in May 1508, and by August had them brought up to the scaffolding installed below half the ceiling. The master was helped by several companions and assistants he had summoned from Florence: they included apprentices from Ghirlandaio's workshop and an old childhood friend, Francesco Granacci.

Michelangelo worked for a year on the first half of the ceiling. In 1509, his more gifted assistants returned to Florence. The pope, a tireless *condottiere*, spent little time in Rome, and Michelangelo found himself struggling not only with the great difficulty of his undertaking, but also with the problem of slow and late payments.

After several interruptions and hesitations, work on the second half of the ceiling was completed in just eleven months, between October 1511 to September 1512. This time, Michelangelo was assisted by only a handful of junior apprentices, who were much less gifted and autonomous than those who had helped him work on the first half of the ceiling. Alone, on a scaffolding nearly 65 feet (20 meters) off the ground, in tortured positions, Michelangelo divided his work into

THE FINISHING TOUCHES

Once the paint dried, Michelangelo, like most artists from the Florentine school, touched up the fresco *a secco* (on the dry surface), correcting errors and darkening shadows and contours.

Lighting

The scaffolding was set above the chapel's windows, blocking all the natural light. Michelangelo worked by candlelight.

The nudes
Set beside the five smaller frescoes of the central narrative, the oak branches and acorns of the nudes represent the powerful Della Rovere family.

THE SISTINE CHAPEL
The lower part of the decoration consists of painted drapery. The twelve frescoes from the fifteenth century are above, followed by a molding on three sides of the chapel that forms an arcade. There are 28 portraits of popes between the twelve windows. On the great vault are found the lunettes and the nine episodes from the Christian Old Testament. On the wall behind the altar: *The Last Judgment.*

larger and larger *giornate.* Every brushstroke counted, since frescoing does not allow for the correction of numerous or serious mistakes. Michelangelo's extraordinary physical strength and immense passion allowed him to challenge the limits of human endurance. The result was one of the greatest masterworks in the history of humanity.

The vault

The first four episodes in the central narrative are from Genesis and tell of the beginnings of creation: 1) *The Separation of Light and Shadows;* 2) *The Creation of the Sun and Moon;* 3) *The Separation of the Earth and the Waters;* and 4) *The Creation of Adam*, one of the most renowned images in the history of art.

THE VATICAN *STANZE*

In Rome, Raphael carried out enormous amounts of work with serenity and grace, traits that won his art the attributes of "divine" and "sublime." He died leaving behind numerous masterpieces and an active workshop.

Along with Michelangelo's frescoes on the ceiling of the Sistine Chapel, Julius II also requested decorations for the *stanze* that Nicholas V had added to the wing of the Vatican palace built 50 years earlier by Nicholas III. The pope no longer wished to live in the Borgia apartments decorated by Pinturcchio and once inhabited by Alexan-

der VI, whom Julius despised. He chose to have the upstairs rooms redone to his taste, though they were hardly shabby quarters, having been frescoed by Benedetto Bonfigli, Andrea del Castagno, and Piero della Francesca, among others. Julius II summoned a number of illustrious artists to decorate "his" rooms: Sodoma Bra-

2

Raphael showed a strong feeling for space and deep love for humanity. As before, he identified goodness with beauty, and proved to be a master colorist. With *The Liberation of Peter* (1), located in the *Stanza di Eliodoro*, he supported the pope's political program, showing that the vicar of Christ was not vulnerable to human attack. In *La disputa del Sacramento* (2), located in the *Stanza della Segnatura*, there are two circles: an upper circle showing the Church Triumphant, and Christ with the Madonna and Saint John surrounded by saints and elders from the two Testaments; and a lower circle showing the Church Militant, with Church doctors, men of letters, and important figures from the artist's time and earlier ages.

mantino, Lorenzo Lotto, and Perugino. Still, when Raphael was introduced to the papal court in 1508 by Bramante, the pope's architect and trusted adviser in artistic matters, Julius II released all the other artists and gave Raphael sole responsibility for the *stanze*. They represented Raphael's first great "official" opportunity.

The program given to Raphael for the first room (the pope's private library, known later as the *Stanza della segnatura* when it was transformed into a tribunal) was inspired by the decorations in older libraries, with depictions of the four faculties of the medieval university—theology, philosophy, jurisprudence, and poetry—all personified as allegorical figures and by symbols in the vault, and illustrated by historical figures and situations.

Inspired by the great importance of this project, and influenced by his direct study of classical Roman statues at the Belvedere, Raphael endowed his work with an overwhelming sense of monumentality—transforming, in effect, the traditional themes that Julius II had assigned to him. The result was the greatest artistic celebration of humanistic culture, a work whose religious and philosophical themes were the supreme expression of papal Rome.

A tribute to Michelangelo

In 1511, the *Stanza della Segnatura* was completed, with its frescoes depicting the *Disputa del Sacramento*, *The School of Athens*, *The Virtues*, and *The Parnassus*. A year earlier, the scaffolding had been removed to reveal the first portion of Michelangelo's frescoes on the Sistine ceiling.

Raphael, though, had probably managed to gain access to the Sistine Chapel before then, gaining some idea of what Michelangelo was seeking to accomplish. The younger artist was apparently overcome by emotion: he immediately erased part of *The School of Athens*, already completed, and placed in the center foreground a portrait of Michelangelo, in the guise of the frowning, introspective philosopher of fire, Heraclitus.

Still, this was not to be Raphael's only tribute to an artist of his time: in the same fresco, also in the center, he painted Leonardo, with his long

The *arriccio*
The first layer of plaster consisted of a one inch (2 cm) layer of lime and volcanic dust.

THE WORKSHOP
Like many contemporary masters, but in contrast to Michelangelo, Raphael worked with a large group of apprentices, to whom he entrusted even delicate tasks.

The "dusting"
By beating a small bag of coal powder against a preliminary drawing with perforated outlines, assistants transferred the forms of various figures to the wall.

The School of Athens
Under Raphael's supervision, an apprentice lay down the final layer of plaster: the *intonachino*.

Perforation
The preliminary drawing was pierced along the outlines of the figures.

blonde beard, representing the great philosopher Plato.

The *Stanza di Eliodoro*

Before starting work on the second Vatican *stanza,* Raphael accepted the offer of the wealthy banker Chigi to try his hand at a large fresco on a classical subject. Though Raphael was effectively "under contract" to the Pope, from whom he received a permanent salary, Julius II and his army had left Rome in 1511 to drive the "barbarians" (Louis XII and his French troops) out of northern Italy. Raphael was thus able to help decorate a hall in the Farnesina villa with a fresco depicting *The Triumph of Galatea.* Upon the pope's return to Rome, though, Raphael immediately went back to work on the *stanze.*

This time, though, Julius II had not returned triumphant: thanks to his Spanish allies, he had indeed attained his goal of freeing Lombardy from the French troops under Louis XII. Still, Julius had almost been deposed during a council convened by the king in Pisa, and he endured a bitter personal defeat in Ravenna. The Spanish, furthermore, had overturned the Florentine republic and brought the Medicis back to power. Julius II could not tell whether this turn of events boded well or ill: however, the Papal States were unquestionably facing a situation of great uncertainty, and he needed to reassert papal authority in no uncertain terms.

Raphael helped Julius achieve this goal. He was asked to decorate the Vatican *stanza* used for public audiences with an explicit representation of

Plato and Aristotle
At the center of the assembly of philosophers, Plato points to the heavens, where he locates the realm of ideas, the foundation of reality. Aristotle turns the palm of his hand toward the earth, persuaded that the order of the universe is to be found in earthly things.

Pythagoras
A boy offers a tablet with the rules of musical proportion to the mathematician who taught that numbers contained the origin of all things.

Euclid
His postulates
form the basis for
Euclidian geometry,
which takes its
name from him.

Socrates
The founder of Western
philosophy made the certainty
of not knowing the basis
of his investigations of man
and truth.

Heraclites
He affirmed the eternal
flux of all things. Raphael
depicted him with the
face of Michelangelo.

Diogenes
He was the founder of
cynicism, which taught that
happiness was to be found
by cultivating indifference
toward earthly things.

The new Saint Peter's
All the great architects of the Renaissance took part in the reconstruction of the basilica: from Bramante to Raphael, and from Baldassare Peruzzi to Antonio da Sangallo the younger.

The tambour
The cupola designed by Michelangelo was to sit upon this tambour.

divine support for the Church throughout its history, and an exaltation of papal politics. Thus began work on the room known as the *Stanza di Eliodoro,* which Julius II, who died in 1513, was never to see in finished form. His successor allowed Raphael to continue work on the decorations, which he concluded in 1514 with the nocturnal vision of *The Liberation of Saint Peter,* emphasizing the futility of attacks against the vicar of Christ.

Leo X

The new pope was Giovanni de' Medici, the son of Lorenzo the Magnificent, who took the name Leo X. An intelligent man, if somewhat lazy, the

Medici pope loved ostentatious luxury, fine food and wine, festivities, hunting, and magnificent ceremonies. He considered Raphael the finest artist of the papal court. Raphael's elegance, his easy relations with the powerful, and his openness had also helped him to advance. His social graces set him in contrast to Michelangelo, who had the additional "defect" of having exalted (in his *David*) the values of the Florentine republic, from which Leo X and his brothers had been exiled.

Leo X, then, esteemed Raphael no less than his predecessor had. He commissioned Raphael to paint the third *stanza,* used for ceremonial dinners, with the *Incendio di Borgo,* as well as the decorations for the Vatican loggias. These two projects were carried out by Raphael's apprentices. Raphael, in fact, was able to do no more than supervise their work, since he had also become superintendent of Roman antiquities, responsible for preventing the destruction of ancient monuments, and also for restoring and preserving what remained. In a sense, then, Raphael was the first archeologist in the history of art. In 1514, he also inherited from Bramante the title of papal architect and the difficult task of supervising the works at Saint Peter's.

This immense amount of activity no doubt took its toll on Raphael's health. He died in 1520, during the night of Good Friday, on the same day he had been born 37 years earlier. The divine Raphael was mourned by all of Rome and by all who had known him, and was laid to rest in the Pantheon.

Raphael's workshop
The decorations for the first loggia (1519), by Giovanni da Udine.

A double portrait
On the facing page, a
portrait painted by

Raphael in 1512. The
character on the left
is the artist himself.

***Portrait of Leo X with
Two Cardinals***
Dating from 1518, this

was the only important
work Raphael
completed for Leo X.

MICHELANGELO'S LATER YEARS

Again, he sculpted for the Medici family. But he was also the architect of their enemies, the Florentine republic. Despite increasing isolation, he dominated the Roman scene. He mounted the scaffolding one last time to create the city's new image.

The supreme effort of the Sistine Chapel frescoes, which lasted nearly 40 years, represented the culmination of Michelangelo's youthful work.

Though he had initially seen the commission as a "deviation" from his primary concern, Julius II's tomb, he overcame his fear of such a enormous undertaking and developed a real passion for the project, making it his very own and even expanding its initial iconographic program. But the time finally came for the man and the artist to return to sculpture, his true voca-

THE MEDICI TOMBS
Commissioned to create tombs for Lorenzo the Magnificent, Lorenzo, duke of Urbino, and Giuliano, duke of Nemours, Michelangelo completed only the latter two projects. He had initially planned a square-shaped monument for the middle of the chapel, but in the end decorated the walls in a sculptural manner.

The tomb of Lorenzo, duke of Urbino

The tomb was created by Michelangelo between 1524 and 1534.

tion, and to the tomb of a pope who had passed away long before, and whose heirs were clamoring for its completion. The saga was destined to continue for many years: between 1513 and 1545, Michelangelo created five different designs for the monument.

In 1513 he sculpted the *Slaves,* whose sketchy forms were just emerging from the marble when Pope Leo X asked Michelangelo to create a facade for the Medici family church, San Lorenzo. (Brunelleschi had left the facade incomplete many years earlier.) Michelangelo, not bothering to disguise his sympathy for the republican cause, returned to Florence in 1516 with the double role of sculptor and architect for the noble family.

But the project was soon set aside— San Lorenzo, in fact, would never have

Michelangelo's facade—when Michelangelo accepted the commission (from the pope and Cardinal Giulio de' Medici) to build a new sacristy for San Lorenzo, to house the tombs of Lorenzo the Magnificent and other members of the Florentine family.

The Medici tombs

Though hardly pleased, Michelangelo could not afford to oppose the wishes of the head of the Church, who enjoyed great influence over noble patrons and rich merchants, and absolute power over Florence. Starting in 1520 (the year of Raphael's death, which greatly aggrieved Michelangelo), he dedicated himself to the realization of San Lorenzo's *Sagrestia Nuova*, a work in which marble statues blend together with columns, niches, and fake windows in *pietra serena* to give life to "architectural sculpture." Marble and *pietra serena*, of course, were the two materials Michelangelo loved most in the world.

He went to Carrara to pick out the stone, but his visits to the Apuan caves seemed to have a negative impact on

SAN LORENZO
In the 1400s, San Lorenzo, an ancient Christian basilica, became the church of the Medici family, who asked Filippo Brunelleschi to work on it.

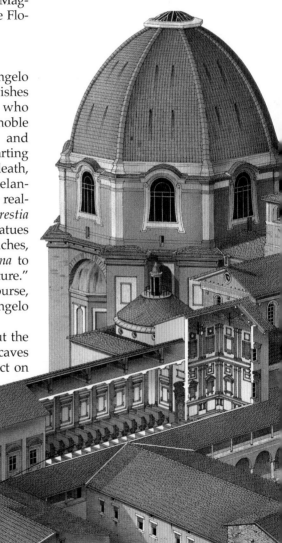

The library
The *Biblioteca laurenziana* houses precious fifteenth-century manuscripts.

**Inside the
new sacresty**
The walls show
not the traditional
decorations, but a
total fusion of sculpture
and architecture.

The new sacresty
It covers an area equal
to that of the old
sacresty, by Brunelleschi.

the evolution of his work. As had happened before—during work on Julius II's tomb and on the facade of San Lorenzo—the carefully chosen marble from Carrara remained untouched. Furthermore, in 1521, the death of Leo X halted work altogether. His successor, the austere Adrian VI, was a Dutchman, whose eminently practical outlook left little room for patronage.

For 22 months (the reign of the Flemish pope), Michelangelo lived in anxiety, relieved only when the cardinal Giulio de' Medici ascended the throne of Saint Peter with the name Clement VII. Michelangelo immediately resumed work on the chapel in San Lorenzo.

The defense of Florence

The period during which Michelangelo attended to this undertaking (1520–1534) were years of great suffering, both in the artist's life and in the political life of the peninsula. In 1521, the Hapsburg emperor Charles V (who had united the German empire and Spain under his rule) took possession of the duchy of Milan, with the help of the pope. Milan was immediately reconquered by the French army, led by François I. His troops, though, were defeated at Pavia by the imperial army (1525). Frightened by Spain's immense power on Italian soil, Clement VII changed sides, in the process drawing

Drawings
Michelangelo combined aesthetic considerations with practical goals in his plans for fortresses. He used zoomorphic forms in place of the traditional geometric ones, which were ill-suited to the new methods of attack.

A rampart

This rampart, in the distinctive form of a crab's claw, was designed but never completed by Michelangelo. It allows shots to be fired from every possible angle.

the emperor's ferocious reprisals upon Rome. In 1527, the city that Michelangelo and Raphael had made the indisputable center of western art was sacked, and the pope was forced to hide in the Castel Sant'Angelo. The Medicis, too, were driven from Florence, and the newly reborn republican government asked Michelangelo to create new defenses for the city, in anticipation of the inevitable reaction by the Medici forces.

In his designs for city gates and ramparts, Michelangelo concentrated on the offensive attacks of the artillery. He sketched out (though never completed) strikingly innovative structures in many different forms, the better to resist enemy fire; curves jutted out, in the form of crab claws that threaten and hurl themselves upon the enemy; ramparts rose up like crabs upon the hill; buildings in the shape of stars allowed shots to be fired from every possible angle. In the end, though, Florence fell after a nine-month assault in 1530. Michelangelo, hunted by the imperial troops, was forced to hide in the city governed by the ruthless Duke Alessandro until Clement VII personally intervened on his behalf. It was also out of gratitude for the pope's efforts that Michelangelo immediately resumed work on the Medici tombs in San Lorenzo.

Models
In the Renaissance, architects began using models to show their proposed creations to patrons.

With the annexation of Siena (1555) and of other Tuscan cities, the duchy gained jurisdiction over a wide area. Duke Cosimo I, with his grand projects in a number of different cities, celebrated his own glory and that of the entire Medici family.

The end of an era

The years that followed were filled with concerns and anxieties for Michelangelo. In 1531, he lost his father, and resulting need to manage his own properties (farmlands in particular) was a burden for him. His sojourns in Rome lasted longer and longer. He was no longer in Florence in 1537 when Duke Alessandro was assassinated by his cousin Lorenzo (known as Lorenzino or Lorenzaccio); young Cosimo de' Medici, from a different branch of the family, assumed control of the government. Cosimo managed to transform Florence from a civic into a regional state, and to some extent helped the city recapture its former artistic and cultural glory.

But he did so without Michelangelo, who was never to return to Florence as a living man. Clement II and all of Rome wished to forget the ransacking of 1527. Artists who were scattered all over Italy were called back to Rome. The pope asked Michelangelo to return to the Sistine Chapel to create an enormous fresco on the wall behind the altar, depicting *The Last Judgment*. Michelangelo returned definitively to Rome in the spring of

The Last Judgment brought the cycle of paintings in the Sistine Chapel to a close: the destiny of man in God's plan, from the creation to the end of time, when the risen Christ rewards the just with the kingdom of heaven, and the wicked with eternal suffering. The story of the last judgment is told in the Gospel according to Saint Matthew, and it became a subject for paintings in the Middle Ages. Michelangelo's fresco is the most renowned interpretation of this theme, and shows once again the master's plastic conception of the human form.

 1534—just a few days after Clement's death. Fortunately, his successor, Paul III of the Farnese family, was a great admirer of Michelangelo and confirmed Clement's commission.

On April 26, 1553, the scaffoldings were already up for the initial preparation of the wall's surface. In the process, two frescoes from the earlier cycle commissioned by Sixtus IV were erased, and a slight incline was created. On May 18, 1536, the 66-year-old Michelangelo climbed up the scaffolding and started work—23 years after he had painted the Sistine Chapel ceiling.

All of Italy was talking about Michelangelo's undertaking; the interest

The risen
Around the angels, groups of risen souls, reunited with their bodies, rise to heaven.

Christ
Christ and Virgin Mary surrounded by apostles, saints, blessed souls, and Old Testament figures.

Angels
Below Christ, the angels' trumpets announce the end of time.

The damned
The damned are flung toward the pit of hell. Many struggle in vain against their fate.

117

and anticipation were unprecedented. Since Raphael's death, Michelangelo had been the most renowned of all artists. By 1540, the upper portion of *The Last Judgment* was completed, and it was then that the scandal of the "nudes" erupted. During an official visit to the chapel by the pope and a group of clergymen, the cardinal Biagio da Cesena, Paul III's master of ceremonies, remarked scornfully that the fresco was fit not for the pope's chapel, but for "a public bath or a tavern." (Michelangelo took revenge by depicting Biagio as Minos.) The pope, nevertheless, asked Michelangelo to complete his work. Because of his great esteem for the artist, he also asked him to take on some of the most important works then being carried out in Rome.

The new Rome

Following the urban renewal that began in the fifteenth century, and was continued by Bramante and Raphael—and despite the many wounds inflicted by the troops of Charles V and their sack—Rome was expanding and being renovated.

Michelangelo was asked to carry out work on a vast scale: from 1538 to 1564, he created the new plan for the Campidoglio and its *piazza;* from 1546 to 1564, he supervised the renovation of

The pavement
The geometric design on the pavement of the *Piazza del Campidoglio* is Michelangelo's work.

Two Romes
The renovation of the Camidoglio hill created a new, vital relationship between ancient, monumental Rome and the new Roman neighborhoods—which had prevously been totally separate areas.

Porta Pia
Commissioned by Pius IV as the main entrance to the city, it was created largely according to Michelangelo's plan. The pediment, though, is a more recent work.

Marcus Aurelius
The equestrian statue of the Roman emperor was placed in the *piazza* in 1532, early in the renovations. It was later moved onto a pedestal designed by Michelangelo.

The completed basilica
The painting is by Louis Haghe, from 1868.

Michelangelo's cupola
Michelangelo's cupola hides the earlier geometric structure. Once again, his decorations and architectural concepts represent a fusion of two arts: sculpture and architecture.

THE PRESENTATION OF THE MODEL
Michelangelo showed his model for the cupola to the pope and his cardinals.

Saint Peter's; from 1561 to 1564, he designed Porta Pia; and from 1561 to 1563, he transformed the ancient baths of Diocletian into the church of Santa Maria degli Angeli.

Michelangelo was usually given *carte blanche* in all his undertakings. In the case of Saint Peter's, though, he needed to take into account the work of his predecessors—who included Raphael, Bramante, and Antonio da Sangallo.

Michelangelo planned to revive Bramante's concept of a church with a central plan—like a pedestal for the great cupola.

He took no risks in drawing up plans, taking as his model Brunelleschi's cupola for the *duomo* in Florence. Michelangelo presented his project to the pope in the form of a large wooden model of half of the cupola. He was never to see the cupola in final form: it was completed at the end of the century, with a few modifications, by Giacomo della Porta and Domenico Fontana.

In his later years, he remained active, devoted himself to charity, and took care of his nephews in Florence.

Michelangelo was 80 years old when he died on February 18, 1564. His remains were brought to Florence, the city he had left 30 years earlier, and laid to rest in the Church of Santa Croce.

Glossary

arriccio: the first, rough layer of plaster laid upon a wall in preparation for subsequent treatment (frescoing, for example).

cantieri: (plural of *cantiere*) any workshop or site for the execution of a work of art, a building, a ship, public works, etc.

condottiere: the leader of a band of mercenary soldiers.

cortile: a courtyard.

fleur-de-lis: an iris or lily, used in heraldry and fine arts as the symbol of the French kingdom and other noble houses.

giornata: the portion of any type of work (often, a fresco) that can be completed in a day *(un giorno).*

intonachino: in frescoes, a second, smoother layer of plaster, laid on the *arriccio,* in preparation for painting.

lavabo: in the Catholic Church, a basin used for ritual washing.

loggia: in architecture, a covered open-air aircade.

palazzetto: a small *palazzo* ("building" or "palace").

piano nobile: the first or second floor of a noble family's *palazzo,* where guests were received.

piazza: a city square. Examples: Piazza San Marco in Venice, Piazza della Repubblica in Florence.

pietra serena: a type of sandstone, sometimes with a blue-gray tint, used for sculpture and other artistic work.

scudi (plural of *scudo):* a type of coin once used in Italy.

segretario: a high public official in Renaissance Italy, whose duties varied from city to city.

ser: a man's title, short for *sere,* roughly equivalent to *Sir, Lord,* or even *Mr.* (for a distinguished but not necessarily noble gentleman).

stanze: the plural of *stanza,* meaning "room" or "hall."

Stanze della Segnatura: a series of rooms in the Vatican, painted by Raphael, once used for legal proceedings (including the granting of pardons) by the popes.

studiolo: a small study (room for reading, writing, and private reflection).

Index